Broadway Christian Church Fort Wayne
And I Look For The Resurrection   WC
Baxter, Kay M.

0000   0347

P9-CCV-079

AND
I LOOK FOR
THE
RESURRECTION

AND
I LOOK FOR
THE
RESURRECTION

Kay M. Baxter

Property of
Broadway Christian Church Library

ABINGDON PRESS

Nashville   New York

PROPERTY OF
BROADWAY CHRISTIAN CHURCH LIBRARY
910 BROADWAY
FORT WAYNE, IN 46802

AND I LOOK FOR THE RESURRECTION

Copyright © 1968 by Abingdon Press

All rights in this book are reserved.
No part of the book may be reproduced in any
manner whatsoever without written permission of
the publishers except brief quotations embodied in
critical articles or reviews. For information address
Abingdon Press, Nashville, Tennessee.

Library of Congress Catalog Card Number: 68-11711

Scripture quotations are from the New English Bible,
New Testament. © the Delegates of the Oxford
University Press and the Syndics of the Cambridge
University Press 1961. Reprinted by permission.

The quotation from *Inadmissible Evidence* by John Osborne, p. 38, is
used by permission of Grove Press and David Higham Associates.

The excerpt from *War and Peace* by Tolstoy, pp. 38-39, is reprinted
from the edition published by Oxford University Press.

The quotation from "Sailing to Byzantium" by William Butler Yeats,
p. 58, is reprinted with permission of The Macmillan Company, Mr.
M. B. Yeats, and The Macmillan Company of Canada, from *Collected
Poems* by William Butler Yeats. Copyright 1928 by The Macmillan
Company, renewed 1956 by Georgie Yeats.

The poem from *The Happy Haven* by John Arden, p. 59, is from
Penguin New English Dramatists, Vol. 5, and is used by permission
of Penguin Books.

The quotation from *Dying We Live,* p. 60, is used by permission of
William Collins Sons & Co.

SET UP, PRINTED, AND BOUND BY THE
PARTHENON PRESS, AT NASHVILLE,
TENNESSEE, UNITED STATES OF AMERICA

MAY WE SUGGEST
SOME WAYS TO USE THIS BOOK

Yes, if you want to use this as a meaningful personal book of Lenten devotions, you will find Kay Baxter's guidance and companionship to be an unforgettable experience. As a matter of fact, you might want to use it that way first.

But then—do read it aloud! Kay Baxter prepared it first for oral delivery at a Good Friday service in a parish church near London—the first lay woman to be invited to do such a thing in an Anglican church. A courageous village rector, The Reverend Canon Edward Hudson, gave up his pulpit to Mrs. Baxter so that this could be read aloud to his congregation.

If you are a parson, you will quickly see that *And I Look for the Resurrection* can be used at any time during Lent; you will also see that a lay reader could be invited to make this presentation to your congregation. Indeed, you yourself, may want to read it to your flock. There is a cadence to it—when you read it aloud.

But be you parson or layman, you will see that this devotion will deepen your awareness of God in the everyday situations of life, and that it is unique in that it draws illustrations from many of the contemporary plays with which you are familiar.

We have designed the book with special care. We have used type that is easy to read aloud in small groups or in the great congregation; we used the church year color of purple to remind you of its meaning for Lent. We hope to have introduced you to an experience that will give depth of meaning to Lent: not to lead

5

you to an observance of the death of Christ—but that you may *Look for the Resurrection.* This is an ageless and eternal experience of Christian faith set in the framework of the contemporary. By reading it and by hearing it, we believe that you will be led to a greater participation in it.

The Publishers

CONTENTS

Introduction 9

I. Father, forgive them 15

II. Today you shall be with me in Paradise 22

III. Mother, there is your son 30

IV. My God, why hast thou forsaken me? 37

V. I thirst 45

VI. It is accomplished 52

VII. Father, into thy hands I commit my spirit 57

Conclusion 63

INTRODUCTION

In these meditations on the Words from the Cross, the illustrations
are taken almost exclusively from contemporary drama. The
objective is in no way to minimize the reality of that act of God
which, on Good Friday, Christians meet to commemorate. Drama
is not make-believe. It is the imitation of an action. Great drama,
like any other great art, explores and presents truth. The truth
upon which Christians concentrate their thought on Good Friday
is the truth about a relationship—the relationship of Jesus, Perfect
Man, to Perfection, and our relationship to that Perfection in our
daily life. The objective in using illustrations from contemporary
drama is to bring to our thinking the help which serious writers
can bring us. Today these writers are grappling in secular language with some of those deep realities of human life which, for
Christians, are spoken of in the story of the Crucifixion—a story
which is the prelude to the Resurrection.

It is customary in writing about Good Friday to set the scene.
The scene is not any local church building. It is a vacant lot outside an occupied capital city. The onlookers are not the inner
ring of today's Christians who habitually observe Good Friday.
They are a crowd more like the crowd at a prizefight. They have
come out to see blood—to enjoy violence. The central figure for
them is not the second person of a trinitarian deity vaguely, or
clearly, accepted as part of a religious system, but a young, exhausted man, thought by some to be the illegitimate son of his
mother; by others, to be a magician; by others, a failed rebel-
leader; now, in any case, at the end of the road—about to die in
squalor and disgrace a very common death. Down through the

9

centuries all over the world, men, women, and children have died in far more prolonged and dreadful ways than the three-hour agony that changed the world; but the world has not been changed by their deaths. So what was this death all about? What led up to it?

The hidden years of ordinary working life, the three years of the manifestation, success and opposition, the healing miracles, the growing tension between the young, itinerant preacher and the establishment, the decision to take the challenge directly to Jerusalem at the Passover Feast, the brief moment of happiness at Bethany, the final conflict, the Last Supper with the friends, the agony in the garden, the betrayal, the trial, the condemnation, the desertion of the disciples, the long journey bearing the cross; the Crucifixion, and now the last minutes of the life of the Son of Man who is also the Son of God—the story is so familiar that it slips from the mind even as one tries to hold it. It is doubtful if any attempted dramatization of the factual events of the Gospels helps at all to illuminate our understanding of what was happening on Calvary, so long time ago. There are valid reasons why, in the 1940's in England, Dorothy Sayers was asked to write for radio *The Man Born to Be King,* and at that time some people who no longer knew the outline of the historical story did, as a result of the labors of writers and broadcasters, gain some knowledge of the historical Jesus as a real, existing Palestinian of the first century A.D., though, even so, it is questionable whether the inevitable artistic tensions between our age and the circumstances of a vanished epoch were satisfactorily resolved in the radio plays. In any case, the time gap is too vast for the historical realities to communicate through any such transient medium. All the people concerned, those who said one thing and those who said another, and all their descendants, are gone, long time ago. Their culture is not ours; the stresses of their lives are not ours. Disease, torture, and death are indeed not unknown to our generation, but the first-century attitudes toward them were widely different from our own; although even then the Jews were divided into those who thought there was a resurrection and those who believed there was nothing after death. We have to try to think what the inner core of the meaning of Calvary is for us *now* and what we mean when we say that Christ died and rose again.

This is not the time to attempt to draw a distinction between the Jewish idea of God and the idea of God held by any particular school of thought among twentieth-century Christians. And it would ill become us to presume to penetrate the interior anguish of spirit undergone by the Savior of the world as his divine nature, locked in a dying skull, in a place called Golgotha, took its way to the God with whom he was from the beginning.

> We may not know, we cannot tell,
> What pains he had to bear.

True—but it is no longer quite easy for many of us to continue Mrs. Alexander's hymn with the words:

> But we believe it was for us
> He hung and suffered there

because those words suggest a legalistic debit and credit account which the modern mind rejects as a symbol for any conceivable relationship between God and man. And our generation has had to face, in situations like the Eichmann trial, the futility of attempting to equate blame and penalty in any universal terms. However, poets, painters, musicians, dramatists, and sculptors are all drawn to this story inescapably because they are aware that it represents some fact—some truth—of profound significance for humanity.

11

There is much modern dramatic writing which, while in no formal sense religious drama, expresses the pondering of man, the deep questioning he experiences, as he faces the ultimate realities of life's suffering, failure, and death—asks himself what may lie beyond and attempts to strengthen his own hope. From studying such work one really can draw understanding of what human life is about and of how people today feel related to or estranged from God. From such writing are drawn the examples in the chapters which follow.

Of course there are many levels on which one may consider the meaning of that withstanding of the Jewish and Roman authorities which led Christ to death. We can appreciate to a certain extent what happens politically to people who refuse on principle to give in to superior force. The French dramatist Anouilh, in his play *Antigone,* has shown us something of the purgative power of resistance to the death, insofar as it concerns the restoration of political health to a community that has been poisoned by lack of coherent moral principle in its government, by the expediency which the Jewish high priests invoked to justify Christ's condemnation. Anouilh wrote this play (based on the Greek story) for the resistance movement in France under the German occupation in 1940. He shows us "little Antigone" defying tyranny in order to honor her obligations to her dead brother. Antigone, in defiance of King Creon's law, steals out in the early dawn and buries her dead brother Polynices—Creon had commanded he should be left unburied, this being a disgrace to Polynices' fame and a denial of his entry into the After World (according to the faith of that age). Antigone faces Creon, and he offers her "happiness." She refuses—refuses love and position and the future with all its joy because she has to honor her obligations.

He tells her that she doesn't understand. She says, "I am not here to understand. . . . I am here to say no to you, and die." And

12

she continues, "Now it is you who have stopped understanding. I am too far away from you now, talking to you from a kingdom you can't get into, with your quick tongue and your hollow heart."

Watching the play, no thoughtful Christian can fail to note the similarities between this scene and the trial scene of the Christ before Pilate. Indeed, as we watch Anouilh's play, we are brought face to face with one of the central questions of Good Friday; we ask with Kierkegaard whether the fatal leveling process of our time can be stopped by the courage of persons accepting an absolute responsibility. This is one, a small one, of the questions that arise from the story of Calvary. It is not that we can equate the Antigone story with the story of the Crucifixion. Antigone does indeed honor her obligation as she and her society saw it. But the Lord's task is other. Antigone's death will not turn the world upside down. Her task is to be *herself*. The task of the Lord is to draw all men to him. Furthermore, the darkness that covered the dead Antigone was the final darkness of death. The darkness that hid Golgotha was, we believe, the darkness that comes before dawn. And the division that separates Christians most sharply from non-Christians, even today when all distinctions tend to be blurred, is that *we* say that if Christ be not risen, then our faith is vain. We do not always face the full implications of this tremendous statement.

Good Friday has no meaning if it is regarded simply as a recalling of the defeat and death of a good man. It is of value to us only if we can, from its observance, gather strength to meet the stern demands of a resurrection faith—a *faith,* not a certainty— a faith that death is the inevitable prelude to any new life whatsoever. Death comes to us in many guises and not always all at once. Paul knew what it meant to die daily. But it comes—and only on the other side of death is the fullness of new life possible. Some of us believe this to be the truth about human existence,

13

and it is because the Christian church helps us to hold and penetrate and face up to this belief that we are Christians and dare to say that we believe in the Resurrection. We must try to understand what conduct such a belief demands from us in contemporary life.

What are the conditions for resurrection in our age? How must we approach the place called Golgotha if any of the words that were spoken there two thousand years ago are to have power over our lives? Let us begin quietly. The hymn "Lead, Kindly Light" may not be to everyone's taste, but at the end of any Lenten season, how many of us can avoid saying as we look back over our feeble efforts, "Pride ruled my will; remember not past years"?

Pride has no place at the foot of the Cross; we have to lay it down. So let us agree that on Good Friday we start by laying down pride and by preparing to face before God the fact that in spite of the two thousand years that separate us, we stand beside those superficially religious Jews, those self-concerned Roman administrators, those callous, hired executioners, those violence-loving local crowds, those inadequate, cowardly disciples.

I

*And when they reached the place called The Skull, they crucified
him there, and the criminals with him, one on his right and the other
on his left. Jesus said, "Father, forgive them; they do not know
what they are doing."*

We must agree that it would ill become us to try to penetrate
the interior anguish of our Lord as he surrendered manhood to
Godhead. But men do, often, die as they lived. The ruling passions
are strong in death, and it is not fanciful to hold that our Lord's
last hours were an epitome of his years of life.

We believe that Christ is the Way, that his life is the pattern
of the life which prepares for resurrection. If we die with Christ,
can we indeed dare to hope we may live with him? What, as
we see them exemplified in our Lord's words from the Cross, are
the conditions for resurrection? What is the road this man
walked down?

Many of us can recall from our own lives some person of heroic
goodness who moved serenely and humbly toward certain death
and whose example strengthened us to tread our own way more
courageously. It is with something of the same intention that we
should set out upon these meditations. *We* do not come to Calvary to be crucified. We come to be strengthened. We all need
courage. Christians, on Good Friday, have a blessed example to
study.

Think first of the climate of the time, the historical climate
of the first century A.D. With all its differences it seems not wholly
unlike our own. Ignorance, fear, violence, and retaliation were the
coin of the realm, so to speak. In his lifetime our Lord offered for

15

ignorance, assurance; for fear, love; for violence, courtesy; for retaliation, atonement.

Coming up to Jerusalem for the Feast of the Passover, Christ had passed all the danger signs that could have warned him to turn back, withdraw the offer, and save himself. On the Via Dolorosa he walked to his death with the offer still open. His world (which is also our world) rejected his offer, and his comment on that rejection was, "Do not weep for me; no, weep for yourselves." The first Good Friday was the day the world decisively rejected the offer Christ made—to bring man to his true humanity, to enable man to recognize who he is.

Many contemporary plays are concerned with questions of identity, and perhaps one of the recent freedom songs deals best with this problem of how a man can establish his identity. It asks how many roads a man must travel before he can claim full humanity, and it goes on to list man's basic needs. The refrain is: "The answer is blowing in the wind." For us the answer is blowing in the wind on a Cross on Calvary where a torn inscription flutters, an inscription which reads "This is Jesus the king of the Jews."

That inscription records the deliberate giving up of a man's own life for the benefit of the lives of others—the true dedication of kingship. Our age has produced many such sacrifices. One has been celebrated by Arthur Miller in his play *Incident at Vichy* in which the plot revolves around the action of a Gentile who, by giving to a Jew his own identification papers, saved the life of the Jew, condemned to the gas chamber, and died in his stead. The same incident, or a variant of it, is used by Rolf Hochhuth as part of his play *The Deputy;* though Hochhuth has expanded the sacrificial action to include two men. Hochhuth's play deals with the question of the pope's share of responsibility in failing to exert pressure on Hitler to prevent the deportation and extermina-

16

tion of the Jews in World War II. It shows that there are still, even in the darkest and most extreme situations of terror and tyranny, men who will sacrifice themselves for others. Gerstein, the German soldier, and Riccardo, the Jesuit priest, have both dedicated themselves to being with the Jews in Auschwitz, even though their action may not save the life or mitigate the suffering of a single Jew. The dedication in Gerstein's case springs from motives of pure human compassion; in Riccardo's, because he is driven so to act that Christ, his master, may have at least one "representative" or "deputy" in the hell to which evil has consigned so many human souls. Our Lord himself has said there is no greater love. Yet these are human transactions; there is another quality in the Lord's action on Calvary.

What is the first condition for resurrection as our Lord's words from the Cross reveal it?

"Father, forgive them; they do not know what they are doing."

We are here brought face to face with the necessity of forgiveness. Children forgive each other more easily than adults do; the word "sorry" comes more easily to young lips than to old. Setting aside the obvious necessity to forgive those who despitefully use us, ourselves—and that's difficult enough—our generation has to face the near impossibility of reaching a full forgiveness in any universal sense. The question arises constantly (the Fellowship of Reconciliation knows this well) of whether we have any right to forgive those who have been and are evildoers to people other than ourselves. We face this problem every time we read of a punitive prison sentence and try to hold in our minds both the damage inflicted on the victims and the disorder of character that the crime reveals in the criminal. How can we hope to enter into the mentality that tortures and then kills small children? However little we really know the darkest sides of our natures, we feel sure that *we* are free of the worst excesses of cruelty, as

17

the daily press brings each morning's quota of beastliness to our breakfast table. But every individual civil crime today is dwarfed by the huge atrocities our generation has perpetrated. We have supped so full of horrors. Auschwitz, Congo, Coventry, Cologne, Hiroshima, Budapest, any police-state, any time, anywhere. Have we any kind of right to forgive such people, and if so, what does forgiveness mean that is not merely weak and culpable indifference? Should it not rather be the duty of Christians to seek out and bring to justice those who have committed the hideous crimes against humanity which our generation has been and is forced to witness? Certainly many noble people who are somehow free of any sense of personal involvement with this evil have felt and do feel this to be their duty, not only from motives of retribution but from a sense that only so will evil be seen to be evil and the younger generation be saved from repetition of equal or worse horror.

Yet this was not the way of Christ. He did not lay upon his disciples the duty of bringing his executioners to book. He did not demand that the disciples judge. Neither does he leave us in the situation where, as a third party to an inflicted evil, he, the Lord, "forgives" suffering which he has not undergone in his own person. Christ's reaction, the overarching forgiveness of love when facing the worst hate could inflict, was silently to absorb the agony into himself and not pass it on except as pure compassion. The body of Christ receives the blows without the shadow of resentment. He takes the blows upon his own body, and there in the timeless perfection of his self-surrender converts hate into love, fear into acceptance. This is impossible? Yes, utterly impossible, except that with God everything is possible, even the two-way traffic of total forgiveness—the preconditions being fourfold. First, the realization that we too could act brutally; then, no cherishing of resentment; third, no passing on of the humiliations and contempt we receive; and fourth, no unrepented sin. We, the church, the body of Christ, are committed to this attempt for life. These preconditions are all we can strive for. And we can generally only strive for them in the trivial, idiotic, banal, boring particularities of our everyday lives, in the small grievances that lurk in our diaries, the small negligences of family and friends, the infinitesimal humiliations that stick like burrs on our ankles till they grow into chains; the imperceptible, repeated choice of self rather than neighbor—the whole horrible tiny bacterial life of sins unrecognized, unacknowledged, unresisted, and unrepented, which hour by hour prepare a situation, a tissue culture, fit for the proliferation of every virulent evil we know in our civilization.

Rolf Hochhuth's play *The Deputy* (though received almost everywhere by the critics as simply an attack on the Vatican's refusal to denounce Hitler's massacre of the Jews in World War II) is, in fact, a deeply penetrating study, in today's terms, of this creeping, insidious yielding to small sins till they grow monstrous. And Max Frisch's *Biedermann and the Firebugs* deals in the satiric mode with the same situation. Frisch shows us a "virtuous" citizen and his wife (with just one small smudge on their beautiful white consciences) who let into their house, out of weakness and stupidity and a desire to be easily pleasant, a criminal who is a firebug. And once he is in, it becomes increasingly impossible to put him outside or to prevent the arrival of his two accomplices. Until in the end they set fire to the house. And all the virtuous householder can do, once he has given them entry, is, to ask at what point *could* he have done otherwise. But if the brood of evil proliferates and grows monstrous wherever it is allowed admission, there is the reverse fact, too often forgotten both by our ethical advisers and by our dramatists. One very small act of atonement, one minute acknowledgment of being in the

19

wrong, the smallest movement of true contrition, has exactly the same power for good as its opposite has for evil. We could, we can, change our world. God, in the Incarnation (a doctrine as central to our faith as is the doctrine of resurrection), gave himself into our hands, weak, infant, at our mercy. Christ grows, or Christ is crucified, at our hands every hour.

And we, the church, are the body of Christ, and share his sufferings. Some who read this know far more painfully than the writer the nature of the crucifixions humanity shares with Christ. Perhaps one of the worst kinds of crucifixion is the cold, callous cruelty of unloving judgments. There is a sort of wall that grows up through the years between two people who once did truly love each other but in whom the need to be *right* has replaced the need to be forgiven. To accept the cold, adverse judgment of a once-loving friend, husband, wife, child, or parent, and not resent it and not pass it on, but remain warm, compassionate, and penitent—this is one of the miracles that grace can accomplish (because with God everything is possible), and where this is achieved, there are the preconditions for resurrection.

The only way to forgiveness of others is our readiness to admit our own need of forgiveness. Our debts *can* really only be forgiven as we forgive our debtors.

Let us pray.

For secret resentments; for preferring self-interest above the interest of the other; for failing to absorb into ourselves the poison of others' hates, others' lies, others' resentments; for all unloving, shallow, and malicious judgments—Father, forgive us; teach us to know what we do.

Praise the Lord, O my soul, and all that is within me praise his holy name. Praise the Lord, O my soul, and forget not all his benefits. Who forgiveth all thy sins, and healeth all thine impurities. Who saveth thy life from destruction, and crowneth thee with mercy and loving kindness.

Let us keep silence.

II

One of the criminals who hung there with him taunted him: "Are you not the Messiah? Save yourself, and us." But the other answered sharply, "Have you no fear of God? You are under the same sentence as he. For us it is plain justice; we are paying the price for our misdeeds; but this man has done nothing wrong." And he said, "Jesus, remember me when you come to your throne." He answered, "I tell you this: today you shall be with me in Paradise."

If the first precondition for resurrection is the two-way traffic of forgiveness, what is the second condition? It is exemplified for us in the story of the two thieves, which it is customary to use as illustration of complacency on the one hand and despair on the other. Augustine's famous "Do not presume; one thief was damned. Do not despair; one thief was saved," is probably its most familiar form. The fierce brevity of Augustine's statement captured the imagination of the playwright Samuel Beckett, and he uses it in the play *Waiting for Godot* to focus attention upon the kind of dilemma modern man faces when he tries to relate the story of the Passion in a literal way to his own daily problems. Beckett's two tramps, Estragon and Vladimir, discuss the fact that the four Gospels differ in their accounts of the thieves, and Beckett makes his two disputants dismiss the topic, after a moment of thought, as being just another of those inexplicable and useless conundrums of theological scholarship on which the learned waste their lives and about which the commoner couldn't care less. And indeed one cannot but agree that a discussion of the discrepancies in the Gospel accounts of the thieves is really just an intellectual puzzle without much relevance to the daily lives of any of us. Why should we be expected to be acutely interested in the fate or reactions of two criminals two thousand years dead when we cannot remember from one day to the next the details of the most recent criminal brought to justice?

Yet the story of the two thieves has exerted, and still exerts, power over the mind and heart of the artist, and over any mind or heart willing to open itself to understanding at a more than superficial level.

For what happened? Two men, *in extremis,* reacted in two quite different ways to their inevitable fate. They were men, we may reasonably assume, whose life histories had been the same confused, directionless struggle against odds as the life history of the ill-equipped, the inadequate, the debased, the perverted, the brutal, who form, as we imagine, our own "criminal class." Several of our playwrights show these types to us now—Rudkin's *Afore Night Come,* Arden's *Sergeant Musgrave's Dance,* Behan's *The Hostage,* Albee's *Zoo Story,* Williams' *Streetcar Named Desire,* and Miller's *Misfits,* among many others. Such plays are often greeted with howls of execration by people who either don't want to, or genuinely don't know, that the world in fact contains a large criminal element, which nevertheless is still composed of men, women, and children made in God's image and therefore of infinite worth however marred that image may be. These plays never give one a cosy evening whether in the theater or beside the television set, but the men who write the best of these plays are serious artists concerned to show what we do to each other and to force our gaze toward the everyday brutalities we inflict on each other. There is, of course, a danger that writers get carried away by indignation or that a cheap mind or a perverted pen writes what should never be written, but we should be thankful that there is so much writing today which is deeply concerned to penetrate to the heart of the matter of our own hate and

23

cruelty and lay bare the roots of evil in us. Graham Greene's plays sometimes show us this kind of situation, and now and then people resent the last-moment conversions some of his characters undergo, feeling that they are hardly convincing and, anyhow, a bit hard on the man trying to be virtuous in everyday life. Yet the Gospel story of the two thieves is quite clear in its statement that a last-moment conversion can happen no matter how desperately wicked the convert may have been; it is, fortunately, not for us to say how this occurs.

But why, of all the crimes in the calendar and all the sins in the decalogue, do the Gospels show us *thieves* as the men crucified with our Lord? The word (malefactors, evildoers) probably covered a wide range of criminality. Yet there is something peculiarly appropriate in the choice of thief as type of all malefactors.

What is a thief? Thieving has two aspects. To thieve is, firstly, to take what isn't yours and, secondly, to deny to someone else what is rightfully his. Thieving comes either from gluttony, from wanting more for yourself than you are prepared to allow to your neighbors, or else from envy, the green-eyed monster which destroys so many otherwise respectable people.

The problem, of course, involves the whole question of the right use of property, the right attitude toward material goods. We are born into a world of materiality; we ourselves are part of that world, and there is true joy to be found in a generous sharing of goods and care for the right spending and the right saving of one's substance; and there are, thank God, many Christians who genuinely and practically regard their possessions as held for the common good and available to common need.

Of course, to give a fair day's work for a fair day's wage is central to the question of honesty at all times, and of course at all times one must resist temptation to the slanderous gossip that steals another human being's reputation. It would be pleasant to be able to affirm to our non-Christian friends that no Christian would dream of smuggling contraband goods through the customs or failing to make an accurate return of tax. These actions are thievish whether we admit it or not.

But there is a deeper dimension of the thieving instinct in our natures, and that is the resentment we so easily feel at being the persons we are, in the circumstances in which we are, to the extent that we feel we have a right to seize for ourselves whatever will give us the edge on our neighbor, whether it is opportunity or reputation or material goods. We take, not because we need but because we want. It is this sort of unwillingness to accept our lot which keeps us keeping up with the Joneses long after all our basic needs are met. As one ages, one learns more about this —perhaps it's one of the particular temptations of age to be inclined to demand things just because the vital fun of being alive begins to lose its sparkle a little. But at this moment of history (when the gap between sheer economic survival and great ease has never been wider—as between East and West for instance), Christians should be particularly committed not to be thieves in this sense—not to take out of the general pool more than is necessary for reasonable living and to examine by pretty rigorous standards what we mean by "reasonable." That is one aspect of thieving—taking for yourself what isn't yours, thievish simply because there are others who need it more and because we are members one of another. This aspect affects us most in the material sphere.

There is a second aspect of this resentment of being what we are, however, and this affects us in the field of human relationship. It leads us to deny to other people what should be theirs in the way of personality. Consider the following example. Gordon Laing's book *The Self and Others* contains a chapter entitled

25

PROPERTY OF
BROADWAY CHRISTIAN CHURCH LIBRARY
910 BROADWAY
FORT WAYNE, IN 46802

"Driving Each Other Mad." In it the author describes several cases known to him where, chiefly through sheer lack of understanding, one human being drives another mad by denying to him or her the right to be himself or herself. Playwrights from Shakespeare in *King Lear* downward have of course often treated this theme, and, in particular, Strindberg in *The Father* has developed a subtle study of what happens to a relationship which goes wrong because of this denial of another person's identity. Many of Tennessee Williams' plays deal with this claiming or denial of identity, and none more painfully than his *Suddenly Last Summer,* which shows a mother's erosion of the personality of her son and the terrible consequences of this upon those the son is involved with. A less well-known inquiry into the same theme is James Joyce's seldom-acted play *Exiles,* where we are shown the complex interrelationship of four people, one of whom, the Joycean "hero," refuses to take responsibility for the interior conflicts of the others and forces them each in turn to face the terrible necessity of accepting the burden of their own freedom—and consequently their own responsibility. It is far easier to "play God" and make other people's decisions for them than to stand back and give them their real freedom. This denial is all too easy to make, especially if one person is in a stronger position than another. It is perhaps the special temptation of teachers and of parents in their relationship to children and adolescents. And when one detects in oneself the desire to manipulate another person—wife, husband, child, friend—the desire to push them into some role that they neither want to play nor are suited to play, then, if one is honest, one has to admit that this is a sort of thieving. One is trying to deny to that person the identity which is his unique possession.

How does one avoid doing this? Let us look again at the Christ, there between the two thieves. Both the criminals are in

very great agony. Both are about to die. Both are utterly im-
mobilized. Neither, one may think, can *do* anything at all either
for himself or for anyone else. One thief reviles Christ, continuing
into death the hate, the resentment, the envy of all that is better
than he, all that is different from himself, which (one has to
suppose) characterized him throughout his unhappy, doomed life.
And why he should have been like that remains part of the
mystery of evil before which we can only be silent. The other
thief? Something, at the very last moment, has happened for him.
At the very last moment the second thief perceives in Christ—
sees with new eyes—a human being so different from any human
being he has ever seen before that he is forced even at the point
of death to think differently about human nature, and therefore
about his own human nature.

This sudden new vision takes him in an odd way. He who (one
may assume) has always looked after number one suddenly
realizes that precisely this is now impossible. He is in a situation
where he can do nothing of himself to help himself. *Only* an
external savior can save him. And though, hitherto, he would
have scoffed at the idea that anyone would be able, let alone
willing, to help him—the despicable outcast he knows himself to
be—yet something in this man on the Cross beside him, as help-
less, as tortured, as doomed as himself, something in Christ's
bearing, even on the Cross, shows the thief the truth—*Ecce Homo;*
this is the man who can save the essential *you* even now if . . . if
. . . if only you will make restitution to him of what you have
denied him. "Restitution? Me? Now? How can I?" "You can."
"Yes. I can. I can give to him what, hitherto, I have resolutely
denied him: the title he rightfully has. The title—my Lord and
my God. This is all I can give. But I give it. I have seen perfection. This man hath done nothing amiss. Lord, when thy kingdom comes, remember me. "And instantly—instantly—the answer

27

Broadway Christian Church Library

from the lips of the dying Christ, the assured word of pardon and reinstatement. "I'll stay with you. You are not alone. You matter." The courtesy of it, the astounding graciousness, the incredible understanding, the unshakable strength! Yet the freedom to choose was given to both thieves right to the end. Our Lord died with them and for them; it was for them to decide how they accepted this death.

Surely the second precondition of resurrection is the willingness to make restitution in any way we can, however late the hour, however hopeless our condition, for the denials we have made, the gluttony, the envy, the resentment we've shown in our lives hitherto, in full recognition of the tremendous gift of free will which makes us fully human. We need have no doubt that we shall be met by the instantaneous pardon of our Lord, the crucified Christ, not from some remote heaven in the future, but today, from where he hangs between two thieves; Emmanuel, God with us, all the way, all the time, now and forever, establishing for us the fact— the only fact that will take away the envy and resentment from our thieving hearts—the fact that we come from God and are going to God, and are, in the sight and love of God, unique, free persons of infinite worth.

Let us pray.

Lord, the problems of world hunger and world loneliness are heavy for us. We do not know what to do. We wish you had not told us that the lonely and the hungry are your brothers and sisters, always, wherever they are. Life could be so much pleasanter if we did not know about them.

Yet save us, Lord, from hardness of heart. Keep us mindful of them, help us to share their gifts, so that it may never be directly through our neglect, our lack of imagination, our greediness, that any one of these, within our power to help, becomes criminal, or that any one of them dies, in body or in spirit, cursing *you* because *we* did not care enough.

Lord, it is only thy grace which can accomplish this work in us. Come like the dawn and light our souls with the flame of thy boundless generosity.

Then Jesus said again, "Simon, son of Jonas, lovest thou me?" "Lord, thou knowest all things; thou knowest that I love thee." "Feed my sheep."

Let us keep silence.

III

Near the cross where Jesus hung stood his mother, with her sister, Mary wife of Clopas, and Mary of Magdala. Jesus saw his mother, with the disciple whom he loved standing beside her. He said to her, "Mother, there is your son"; and to the disciple, "There is your mother"; and from that moment the disciple took her into his home.

Two conditions for resurrection as shown in our Lord's words from the Cross, then, are first, forgiveness, and second, giving to each his due whether materially or spiritually. The Third Word is frequently treated on Good Friday as being the Word which applies to home relationships, and so, of course, it can rightfully be treated. Yet it can be seen in a very much wider context if we care to look. It can be looked at in the whole context of the social gospel, and this is a field where the modern dramatists are very much involved. Dramatists are concerned today very deeply with the true meaning of social responsibility. Harold Pinter's play *The Caretaker* poses quite categorically the question whether, or not, any man is rightfully his brother's keeper, and further, whether, and in what terms, we can attempt to look after the failures in our society. The play shows us three characters. Mick, a quick-witted technician, owns a ramshackle house in need of repair. He dreams of doing it up in expensive style to match a fantasy of gracious living culled from the glossy magazines. His brother Aston also lives there, by Mick's permission, inhabiting one room in the attic, a room filled with every kind of junk. Aston has been hospitalized and has had too much electric shock treatment, and this has left him with nothing of his own personality except total recall of the treatment and a vague, drifting intention,

30

or hope, that one day he may build a shed in the backyard. The third of the trio is a vagrant who answers to the name of Davies, though that may or may not be his real name. His identity is in doubt; he believes, or says be believes, that there are "papers" which would prove who he is, but how can he get them when they are miles away, and he has no decent boots? When he is given a pair of boots, he at first rejects them because they haven't the right sort of laces (no one likes receiving help, really), and in the end he makes excuses not to set off on his journey. Any shelter is better than the open road. The tension which, as always in Pinter's plays, keeps our interest at stretch is achieved here by the fear that Mick may at any moment show the violent side of his nature and either turn the two inadequates out or do them some physical harm.

All three are shown as unable to communicate with one another, partly through fear and partly through the hold which fantasy has upon them. But throughout, Pinter is putting to us the question: "Who should be—who is competent to be—the caretaker of these damaged and inadequate characters, and what are we justified in doing to each other with the techniques of modern scientific medicine in order to achieve conformity to established social norms? Who is my brother? Am I his keeper?"

In his trilogy *Chicken Soup with Barley*, *Roots*, and *I'm Talking About Jerusalem* Arnold Wesker, writing from within the close-knit pattern of Jewish family life, shows us how as understanding deepens, people learn that putting the family first may be all right for a start—charity may (indeed must) *begin* at home —but it must by no means stop there. Men and women have wider duties. Our Lord, we shall remember, rebuked those who wanted him to restrict his ministry to his own people, and when his disciples came to tell him that his mother and his brothers were asking for him, he replied, " 'Who is my mother? Who are

31

my brothers?' " These (among whom his life was cast), *these* are my mother and my brothers. The words read cruelly curt in the Gospel, but one has to recognize that from the time he was twelve years old and stayed behind in the temple at Jerusalem, Christ gave clear evidence that he knew himself called to a public ministry and that the claims of family could not be paramount. And indeed his own celibacy must have been part of his dedication to a wider family commitment—as it still is for those who enter religious orders. Fathers and mothers know well the pain involved in letting go of the beloved son who responds to a vocation which removes him from the intimate family circle. The sword that pierced the heart of Mary is only too familiar to parents.

Yet, though we recognize the probability of partings, no amount of preparation ever really prepares us for the agonizing shock of the death of a beloved person. No one pondering upon the death of Christ could fail to grieve for the suffering of his bereaved mother and the friends who by his death lost their hero, their friend, their leader. Each soul's griefs are private and each different, but most of us who are adult know well how bitterly hard it is to bear the finality of death. The very language people use—our avoidance of the direct word—shows the pain with which we confront the fact of death when it invades our own hearts. It is very far from Christian to attempt to slur over the awful solemnity of death or to pretend that Christians can or should suffer any less than others do from the final separation, in this life, from those through whom we have learned all we know of love. However sure our faith, when our beloved die we weep for their bodily presence, and if we did not, we would be less than human.

Too often when we are happy ourselves, we may shrink from being with the bereaved in a quiet and unforced presence; it is too painful, and we make a variety of excuses not to be the person who stands besides the bereaved one at the foot of the cross. And when grief strikes us, we tend too often to withdraw into a cold, dumb, isolated misery, refusing the timidly proffered hand and letting pride support us if it can.

Our Lord's way is other. He knows we need each other's help. He makes it natural, right, simple that human beings should in their darkest hours support and be supported by each other. One can't *do* much. But one can *be* there. Our Lord's word takes us out beyond the limits we would like to set in this connection. Apart from the fact that in Christ's extreme agony his habit of selflessness persists and he can still think of others—can still think of his mother and his closest friend and see that each could be helped by serving the need of the other, and that's miracle enough —yet the form in which this Word comes to us indicates a vast step forward in the way in which we are presented with our responsibility for each other. To the man Christ says, "There is your mother"; to the woman, "Mother, there is your son," and in these brief phrases all the limits and hedges and barriers that keep us apart in social separation are swept away. A man in need is my son. A woman in need is my mother. Each woman as much to be honored as the woman who bore me, each man as much my brother as the son she bore. The question of the blood tie, or the tie of locality, or the tie of nationhood or race or religion or social class simply is not relevant.

It may be overoptimistic, but there is some ground for believing that, at least among the young, there is a growing understanding of our universal kinship, and that this understanding is gradually shaking the traditional nationalistic reserves of the older generation, the tradition that man is not called upon, usually, to lower the drawbridge and let in the stranger. The young teach us in this matter. They do really feel themselves to be in a brotherly and sisterly relationship with the young of other

33

nations, other creeds, other colors. This is shown very clearly in the popularity among young people of the freedom songs, songs such as:

> If I had a hammer
> I'd hammer out danger
> I'd hammer out warning
> I'd hammer out freedom
> I'd hammer out *love* between the brothers
> and the sisters
> All over this land.*

Or if an example is sought from the legitimate theater, what better example than the part of Katrina in Brecht's play *Mother Courage*? There, though Mother Courage herself personifies all the brutalizing effects of war and is purely self-interested, Brecht has given her a dumb daughter Katrina, a most moving image of selflessness. Toward the end of the play, when the audience is getting worn down by the horrible self-centeredness of everyone in the play, there comes the beautiful, wholly unsentimental sacrifice that this daughter makes to save some children in a besieged town. Katrina, dumb from shock (and none too bright from birth), learns from the casual talk of some soldiers that the invading army is going by night to sack and burn a city across the valley. Horrified at the thought of the death of innocent people, especially children, Katrina determines to rouse the sleeping town. To do this she has no means but a hammer and a drum. She is alone. There is no one who would aid her. She beats on the drum with her hammer till a bullet from the soldiery silences her and she falls dead. But her act has roused the sleeping towns-

* "If I Had a Hammer" (The Hammer Song). Words and music by Lee Hays and Pete Seeger; © Copyright 1958 and 1962 Ludlow Music, Inc., New York, N. Y. Used by permission.

people—people who mean nothing to her except that she alone of all the characters of Brecht's imagination *has*

> . . . *love* between the brothers and the sisters
> All over this land.

There is one more point to make, and it takes us back to the bereavement of Mary the mother and of the disciples. Jewish opinion was divided about resurrection. And Christian opinion is divided about prayers for the dead. Yet there is deeply rooted in many Christian hearts, as in many hearts which worship no god, a terrible, heavy sense of lostness and forlornness when a beloved dies. To meet and to counter this utter emptiness various religions have developed various rituals and ceremonies. We should not be ashamed to admit it if any of these help us in our own time of mourning. Nor, I believe, should we hesitate to admit our own uncertainties or our own lack of faith, if we do lack faith in any future life we can hope to understand in any logical way.

Ketti Fring's play *Look Homeward, Angel,* based on Thomas Wolfe's novel, presents most poignantly the cry of someone experiencing this lostness and at the same time the *need* to pray to— to whom? The younger brother in the play, whose adored elder brother Ben has died after a long illness, is left alone on the evening of the death, his relatives having withdrawn into their own unhappiness without much thought for the remaining boy. Suddenly the weight of sorrow breaks over him, and in a moment of desperate, but unselfish, need to express his longing for Ben's safety, he cries out to the God he does not know, "Whoever You are, be good to Ben tonight." The cry is probably as near to true intercession as anything on any stage at this time.

So then the third condition for resurrection must be our acceptance of membership in the body of Christ from whom the whole family in earth and heaven is named; and when one member suffers, there must always be others prepared to share that suffering, to stand beside the sufferer at the foot of the Cross.

Let us pray.

Let us pray for unity among men and nations.

O God and Father of all, whom the whole heavens adore, let the whole earth also worship thee, all kingdoms obey thee, all tongues confess and bless thee, all sons of men love thee and serve thee in peace, through Jesus Christ our Lord.

> For all wandering men,
> For men with a cross,
>   For men forgetful,
> For sinners, known and unknown to us,
> For those who have broken our hearts,
> Whose hearts we have broken:—
> Teach us thy will.
>   Teach us.

Behold how good and joyful a thing it is, brethren, to dwell together in unity.

O pray for the peace of Jerusalem.

They shall prosper that love thee.

Peace be within thy walls and plenteousness within thy palaces. For my brethren and companions' sake I will wish thee prosperity. Yea, because of the house of the Lord our God, I will seek to do thee good.

Let us keep silence.

IV

At midday darkness fell over the whole land, which lasted till three in the afternoon; and at three Jesus cried aloud, "Eli, Eli, lema sabach-thani?", which means, "My God, my God, why hast thou forsaken me?"

One must repeat that it would ill become us to attempt to pene-trate what happened in the soul and mind of the dying Christ. At this point it is hard to avoid the grossest impertinence. And the dramatists from whom we have been drawing illustrations do not help much here. Yet there is a powerful passage in John Osborne's *Inadmissible Evidence* which may throw light on the nature of despair in our own case. In this play Osborne shows us Bill Maitland, a lawyer, middle-aged, and, in his own words, "irredeemably mediocre." The form of the play is, in effect, a confession of life spoken by Bill, as defendant, to an unseen, silent judge. This very ordinary man goes through, episode by episode, the various aspects of his relationship with those who have made up his business, professional, and family circle—his wife, his daughter, his colleagues, his employees, and his clients. He has failed in all his undertakings, and he says of himself that he never hoped or wished for anything more than to have the good fortune of friendship, and the excitement and comfort of love, and the love of women in particular . . . with friendship, with love, . . . he is not equal to any of it. But he can't escape it. He can't forget it: and he can't begin again.

As the play proceeds, one realizes that one is watching a human soul being devoured in turn by each of the seven deadly sins—pride, lust, envy, sloth, avarice, gluttony—and through them all,

37

anger, anger at life that has dealt him such a hand and at those who uncaringly live out their lives over against him, using him only as a means for their own resentment or release. It is a terrible presentation of absolute despair and goes on to the heartrending end when, his sins and his crimes having caught up with him, Bill Maitland telephones his wife and says: "Do you think I should come home? . . . I don't think there's much point, do you? . . . The Law Society or someone" will find me. Love and law are here sharply contrasted in the negation of hope.

Osborne shows us human despair, and this is terrible, and this is our fault. But in the death of Christ the truth goes beyond what can be represented, and, to my mind, no conventional modern Passion play has contributed anything to our understanding here, though again the study of Samuel Beckett's work, both in *Waiting for Godot* and in *Endgame,* enlarges the understanding of man as he faces his own solitariness.

Yet one can find help from writers. Let us turn to Tolstoy, to *War and Peace,* for the kind of illustration we need, without impertinence, to convey something of the *scale* of the event we are thinking about—the scale of the sacrifice of Christ. *Something* of what is needed is contained in Tolstoy's description of the wounded Prince Andrew Bolkónski, a character around whom Tolstoy built up a good deal of his own inquiry into the essential attributes of love and its relationship to death. Tolstoy describes the wounding of Andrew Bolkónski, who is left for dead on the field of battle, thus:

On the Pratzen Heights, where he had fallen with the flagstaff in his hand, lay Prince Andrew Bolkónski, bleeding profusely and unconsciously uttering a gentle, piteous, and childlike moan.

Toward evening he ceased moaning and became quite still. He did not know how long his unconsciousness lasted. Suddenly he again felt that he was alive and suffering from a burning, lacerating pain in his head.

"Where is it, that lofty sky that I did not know till now, but saw today?" was his first thought. "And I did not know this suffering either," he thought. "Yes, I did not know anything, anything at all till now. But where am I?"

He listened and heard the sound of approaching horses, and voices speaking French. He opened his eyes. Above him again was the same lofty sky with clouds that had risen and were floating still higher, and between them gleamed blue infinity. . . .

[Hoofs stopped near him. It was Napoleon, who was riding over the battlefield, looking at the killed and wounded. He stopped before Prince Andrew.] "That's a fine death," said Napoleon as he gazed at Bolkónski.

Prince Andrew understood that this was said of him and that it was Napoleon who said it. . . . But he heard the words as he might have heard the buzzing of a fly. Not only did they not interest him, but he took no notice of them and at once forgot them. His head was burning, he felt himself bleeding to death, and he saw above him the remote, lofty, and everlasting sky. He knew it was Napoleon—his hero—but at that moment Napoleon seemed to him such a small, insignificant creature compared with what was passing now between himself and that lofty infinite sky with the clouds flying over it. . . . So insignificant at that moment seemed to him all the interests that engrossed Napoleon, so mean did his hero himself with his paltry vanity and joy in victory appear, compared to the lofty, equitable and kindly sky which he had seen and understood, that he could not answer.

[He wishes he could pray to the God his sister believes in, but he cannot.] "There is nothing certain, nothing at all except the unimportance of everything I understand, and the greatness of something incomprehensible but all-important."

In this passage, which is abbreviated considerably, Tolstoy shows us the withdrawing of a spirit as it approaches death from all that is imperfect and transient in the physical sphere, all this that seems like "the buzzing of a fly"; he shows us how all ambitions fade and shrink beside the supreme, incomprehensible reality of the ending of life here on earth.

The great mystical writers take us a stage further and show us how the soul may be led into an area of experience where even the things of the spirit—the sure holds, the climber's crampons—are gone, and sheer void is above and below. It is described by many poets. Let one passage by Walt Whitman suffice. Whitman writes this about the way which leads the soul, darkling, to God.

> Darest thou now, O Soul,
> Walk out with me toward the Unknown Region,
> Where neither ground is for the feet, nor any path to follow?
>
> No map, there, nor guide,
> Nor voice sounding, nor touch of human hand,
> Nor face with blooming flesh, nor lips, nor eyes, are in that land.
>
> I know it not, O Soul;
> Nor dost thou—all is a blank before us;
> All waits, undream'd of, in that region—that inaccessible land.

"I know it not, O Soul." No, we do not really know it. But Christ does. And his mystics and saints do too. St. John of the Cross writes this about the discipline which brings the human soul to God:

The soul is conscious of a profound emptiness and destitution of the three kinds of goods—natural, temporal and spiritual. The *sensual part* is purified in dryness, the *faculties* in the emptiness of their powers, and the *spirit* in the thick darkness. . . . It is like being suffocated or hindered from breathing. But this contemplation is also purifying the soul, undoing or emptying it, or consuming in it, as fire consumes the rust and mouldiness of metal, all the affections and habits of imperfection which it had contracted in the whole course of its life.

How different from the experience of a Bill Maitland! One can only believe that the reason Christ, the sinless one, underwent this experience is because he willed to be fully human. Out of this thick darkness—symbolized in the Gospels by the darkness over the land—Christ uttered the cry of dereliction which even now makes the heart stand still.

For (in our ignorance we ask) if this can happen to God's sinless Son in a world God made, *what kind of God are we worshiping?*

That is the sort of question our non-Christian friends put to us, and it is hard to find words in which to speak about our faith at this point.

Are we back in the Old Testament with the God who tormented his servant Job simply to win a bet with the devil? Indeed, this is the reaction of many people to that tremendous, existentialist poetic drama. Or are we forced to see at this moment the Christ as Albert Schweitzer is said to have described him—a heroic man who thought he could change the world, and, when he found he could not turn the wheel alone, flung himself upon it and was broken in the process? Did Christ really expect *not* to die? Is the author of the *Passover Plot* right, and was the intention that he should appear to die (as the result of drugs) but that he should in fact be rescued in the nick of time—the intention being unaccomplished when he was not rescued?

So many great scholars and great saints all down the centuries have thought and written about this that one would be foolish indeed to think one could contribute anything to knowledge here. But a certain number of people have found down through the

41

years of their own lives that this cry of dereliction is utterly central to their faith as Christians and to their belief in the Resurrection: and this for two reasons. First, because the recording of the cry disposes of the claim that the Crucifixion was a mythical, legendary event in which a god, like one of the Greek gods, took human shape for a short while on earth and went away when he'd had enough. No—this is how a man dies—this is how you or I may die. In darkness. The God we worship is an incarnate God. Dying, Christ did not abandon his faith in the creative spirit he knew as Father. He continued into death the practice of his whole life— the practice of turning to God for everything. Entering into our ignorance (like us, dare we say at this moment, unable to understand the absence and the darkness), he does not curse nor cry to the onlookers nor rail against fate. He asks the question we all ask at some time or other—*"Why* are you doing this to me?" And there is no answer.

> Christ leads me through no darker rooms
> Than he went through before.

One of the conditions for resurrection is that we accept our creaturely ignorance and the "dullness of our blinded sight"; in our own small way, knowing that by accepting ignorance we share, however limitedly, in the darkness of Christ. This is the first strong cord that binds us to belief in the truth of the Passion story. The second is one more concerned perhaps with the professional eye of a writer and may not be relevant to everyone, but it shall, nevertheless, be mentioned.

Much doubt is cast by scholars on the authenticity of the Gospel records—written long after the event, written from within a different culture, not coherent one with another, and so on. The arguments are many against believing factually what the New Testament tells us.

There is, however, one aspect of this kind of criticism which seems to support, rather than threaten, personal faith. It is this. The men who set down what happened on Calvary set down the cry of the dereliction of Christ, the cry of "forsaken!" With all the dangers they must have recognized (the risk of showing up the whole story as being the story of a misguided reformer who made a big mistake and paid for it with his life), they *set it down*. To do so is the action of truthful witnesses. It is these same witnesses who also tell us Christ rose again. Why should we not believe them?

Let us pray.

Let us pray for all who suffer desolation and are tempted to despair.

O blessed Lord, Father of mercies, Spirit of comfort, make us thy ministers of hope to our fellow human beings. Give us courage to uphold them when they are distressed. Help us to assure them that there is no darkness where thou art not. Strengthen, in the merciful service of psychiatry, the doctors and nurses and social workers who bring relief and care to those whose despair has roots deep in the past or in disease of body. Deliver us from that fear of life which only love can allay, and suffer us not for any pains of hell to fall away from thee, the source of all life and love.

George Herbert's words may be ours as he prays for "care and courage" to fight despair.

43

O help, my God, . . .

dissolve the knot,
As the sun scatters by his light
All the rebellions of the night.
Then shall the powers which work for grief
Enter Thy pay,
And day by day,
Labour thy praise and my relief;
With care and courage building me
Till I reach Heaven, and, much more, Thee.

Let us keep silence.

V

After that, Jesus, aware that all had now come to its appointed end, said in fulfilment of Scripture, "I thirst." A jar stood there full of sour wine; so they soaked a sponge with the wine, fixed it on a javelin, and held it up to his lips.

We have considered the first three preconditions for resurrection. The need for forgiveness, the need to give to each his due, the need to recognize relationship and responsibility and to share each other's suffering beyond the limits of the blood tie. And having thought about these three, which deal mainly with our life among our fellows, we have attempted to enter a little into the meaning of Christ's sense of dereliction as recorded in the Gospels.

Now we reach what is perhaps the hardest of the Seven Words to speak about because it is so easy to read into it far more recondite and complex meanings than the words really can carry. One has to accept the literal fact that this is the natural agonized plea for human help which any person dying in physical pain may utter.

Thirst was only one of the hideous pains endured by those who were crucified. It is perhaps the only one that can be spoken of in public and in cold blood and may, for that reason, be the only one of the physical sufferings recorded. Anyone who knows the truth about death by hanging needs no reminder of the barbarity of the "due course of justice" as it took its victims even almost up to our own day in "civilized" countries. And no good purpose is ever served by dwelling upon physical suffering in situations where we ourselves remain uninvolved and where we can do nothing to alleviate the suffering.

The Gospels are properly reticent at this point, and it is only when religious art and literature are in a decadent phase that the physical suffering of the Savior is allowed to obscure the work of salvation. Those who know the *St. Matthew Passion* know well how Bach controls the emotions his theme arouses, so that the wild pain expressed by a soloist is almost immediately disciplined by the formal dignity and power of the more impersonal chorales. If you are going to retell the story of Calvary as some dramatists writing for church production have tried to retell it, you have to tell it in very dispassionate language—in such words as, "And sitting down, they watched him there," or you risk sentimentalism and, almost, sadistic and pornographic writing. Yet, without impropriety, there are simple things that can be said which do not risk falsifying or overplaying the emotions we feel at this point.

First, we should note the fact that Christ asked for help. Some of us find it very difficult to ask for help. And indeed one of the problems posed by the complexities of our social structures is the problem of how, and how much, to offer help and how and when to ask for help.

Our Lord knew well that it is more blessed—happier—to give than to receive, and many of us hate having to receive help from anyone, even from those with whom love is so close a bond that it is hard to know who gives and who takes. When the Lord washed his disciples' feet, Simon Peter very much disliked having to receive this service from his Master. And many of us suffer great and quite needless mental pain, in addition to any physical suffering that comes our way, when we have to admit our weakness and our need for care and support from others. This anxious feeling is wrong; if one tries to discover what it springs from, it may well prove that unwillingness to admit fatigue, pain, or dependence stems from two underlying fears, neither of them very creditable to the self. First, we fear that if our friends know that we can't cope, we shall be forced to step down from the image we have made of ourselves as competent, as persons who help others, step down to play the far less attractive roles of persons who are incompetent, inadequate, tiresome, the ones who have once again come unstuck. One of the cruel jibes the crowd hurled at the crucified Christ referred precisely to this situation. "He saved others, but he cannot save himself." It's *his* turn now.

And arising from this there is another unflattering self-discovery, namely, that we do not by any means always love those who come to our rescue when we are in distress. Any social worker knows about this. The truth is universalized and exemplified in the Scriptures, of course, in the story of the ten lepers. Ten were healed; only one came back to say thank you. The crowd—the mob (and we are among the crowd)—dislikes having to feel gratitude. A third discovery we may make is that we fear that if we fall on hard times, we shall find that people we thought were true friends simply fade away; we just lack trust.

All this is no more than to say that all the pains that are natural to being human are intensified and made harder to bear by the inhumanity and grudgingness of men and women to each other, by our lack of generosity, by our meanspirited fear of being under obligations to each other, and by the ungenerous temper which vents itself in the kind of jeer, and sneer, and pleasure in the ill fortune of others which the crowd vented on the Christ as he hung on the Cross. And we don't help the situation if, when we *are* in a position to be of help to each other, we keep a close and well-remembered tally of the helpful acts we have been able to perform for Miss So-and-So and Mr. Such-and-Such!

Yet the Gospel story does not leave us without hope even for our selfish selves. The penitent thief, even dying, did defend Christ's honor; the bystander in the crowd did fill the sponge with sour wine and put it to the dying lips to moisten them. There is never a situation in which some gleam of decency, some ray of human pity doesn't stir.

> For mercy has a human heart
> Pity, a human face.

And it is at this point that we may thankfully acknowledge our kinship with, and our indebtedness to, all those who act generously and spontaneously to relieve suffering out of pure human kindness, though they do not profess the Christian faith or, indeed, any faith, and though they think that we, who do, are deluded. "Lord, when was it that we saw you hungry and fed you, or thirsty and gave you drink?" They may well ask this: but the Lord of all life told us that it is they who will hear the words, "You have my Father's blessing; come enter and possess the kingdom."

There is a good deal of contemporary dramatic writing which explores this willing or unwilling exercise of personal care and its effect in reconciling or alienating people from each other. Graham Greene's play *The Living Room* shows us the dark side through two devout old aunts and a crippled priest-uncle who fail utterly to slake the thirst for love of their young orphaned niece Rose, who is sent to their home. When Rose takes her own life, there is still little real sense that her elders understand their own failure toward her.

Edward Albee's recent play *A Delicate Balance* shows, as Albee frequently shows, a society struggling for human compassion, thirsting for understanding, and solacing this thirst, or trying to solace it, by recourse to the gin bottle or the vodka decanter. Albee leaves us in little doubt what his characters are doing when they drink so continuously. They lack all access to any "living water" or even to the "milk of human kindness." Why do we deprive each other of what any truly human being can supply to another? Where do we find the strength to speak the truth to each other, still in the bond of love?

There is finally one more aspect of thirst about which one must try to speak—thirst of another sort than our common human need for each other's affection and care. It is a thirst for God. "As the hart panteth after the water brooks, so panteth my soul after thee, O God. My soul thirsteth for God, for the living God." Psalms and poems all down the ages are full of this longing, and most of us have experienced, intermittently, something of the desire the poets express.

One would have thought this, at least, was something our Lord would not have had to endure—that his oneness with God would have meant that he at least could say to the end, "He leadeth me beside the still waters." Yet he has known this suffering, and we know *we* suffer this kind of thirst. Only sometimes we don't recognize it for what it is. And so we try to cope with it by secondary means, by pursuing small personal successes, by interior evasions, by refusal ever to be alone, by being too busy to notice —sometimes by taking to drugs or tobacco, to fast cars, to bridge, or simply to drink of another kind. The evasions never work, but we keep on trying.

The most vivid theatrical presentation of this universal thirst is given us again by Samuel Beckett, and again with no direct religious reference, in his mime play *Act Without Words*. Here, on a bare stage a man is seen, and from the wings, or from the flies above him, a glass of water appears and is withdrawn; a large leaf promises shade but does not provide it; a whistle offstage promises the arrival of another person, but no one comes. The entire "act" consists of the man's reactions to the possibility of slaking his thirst or of finding shade from heat or human compassion. In the end he refuses to try anymore. In its strange mixture of farce and tragedy the "play" stirs deep emotional forces in the audience. It offers no solution. Man is solitary. No one cares. He is in need, and he is tormented by an unseen silent force. And that is all.

The story of Calvary is less stark. There *are* other human beings, and one or two of them do care—a little. But the thirst after God can be satisfied only by union with God.

Let us pray.

Let us confess honestly to God that we are tired of being chased around.

O God, please listen. This anxiety, this craving for something we can't define,—does it really come from you? Couldn't you be a bit more explicit, Lord, so that we could know what is really asked of us?

We do love you; at least we want to love you. It's all very well for Augustine to say that "our hearts are restless till they rest in thee," but what does this mean in practice, and how are we to be sure that all this turmoil and dissatisfaction aren't due to something chemical—something a pill could cure? The distance between you and us is so vast, Lord—who can bridge it? O God, please help.

And then let us pray in the quiet confidence of the psalmist.

My soul is athirst for God, yea, even for the living God.
When shall I come to appear before the presence of God?

Why art thou so troubled, O my soul,
And why art thou so disquieted with me?
O put thy trust in God
For I will yet thank him, which is the help of my countenance,
and my God.

Let us keep silence.

VI

Having received the wine, he said, "It is accomplished!"

Mark tells us it was "a loud cry." John tells us what the words were; in the Greek it is one word, *Tetelestai!* "It is accomplished!"

One meets determination in many guises. A small girl, five years old or so, was standing at a table on which was a very dull jigsaw puzzle, endless stretches of gray sky and blue-gray sea, impossibly difficult for a five-year-old. Her grandfather suggested she might give up and do something gayer. The little creature exploded with shock and indignation. "Give *up?*" she said. "Now? Before it's finished? How could we? We've begun it!" That beautiful and rare determination that will not even consider the possibility of defeat is the kind of fiber we pray for as we stand before the Cross. We can call up from our own experience some souls of heroic mold who simply never knew when they were beaten. The schoolboy with the withered leg who became a flyweight boxing champion; the college failure who plodded on through night classes to get the credits he had to have to become the teacher he knew he was meant to be; the Jewish woman social worker who went ten times back into Germany in 1939-40 on secret journeys to bring Jewish children to safety in Britain; the woman in the iron lung who earns a living by her power-driven pen; the blinded man who runs his own hotel; the paraplegic victim of a road accident who just sticks it out in a wheelchair— all the host of the brave who, in T. S. Eliot's words, "are only undefeated because [they] have gone on trying." We all know at least one of that silent army, as well as of the even larger army of those who take on and carry, without ever referring to it, the anxiety and exhaustion of looking after the very aged, the very infirm, the heavily handicapped who exist, alas, in almost every family in the land. We do not always remember how clearly these bear the mark of being the brothers and sisters of the crucified Christ.

Yet the cry "It is accomplished!" is not only the expression of endurance in its painful sense. It is also the cry of the strong warrior, the great athlete—at the last throw of the javelin, at the overcoming of the loneliness of the long distance runner, at the ascent of the sheer face of the mountain peak. It is the cry of a whole man, a grown man, the same man of whom Luke reports that he "exulted in the Holy Spirit"—a man who has fought the good fight, kept the faith, finished the course, done something worthwhile, and done it with all his powers.

These are obvious comparisons to make with the exhausted yet triumphant cry of "accomplished!" which our Lord uttered at the point of death. Yet if that were all, it would be hardly more than Archimedes' cry of *Eureka*—"I have found it!" And it is, of course, worlds beyond that. It is the cry of the victor-victim— victor because victim. And it speaks of the accomplishment of the chosen aim. If we seek examples from the common lives of men dedicated in their aims, it is perhaps from among today's men of science that we are most likely to find outstanding personalities.

Yet the dramatist, often a little farther ahead than we ourselves are, has pinpointed for us the real sword of division in this problem of aims and accomplishments. The Swiss Friedrich Durrenmatt, author of many plays, has written two which especially deal with the scientific working out of aims chosen deliberately and deliberately accomplished. The first play, *The Visit,* describes a woman, now old, who returns to avenge herself on the village which drove her, as a girl, away from it in disgrace. Her life has been, quite literally, hellishly successful. The lover because of whom she was driven out has remained in the village—a very poor small shopkeeper—and she, in the power fabulous wealth has given her, breaks the village and the villagers, forcing them to kill the man who ruined her. It is a ferocious example of evil aims planned with scientific precision and evilly accomplished, and one sees the hideous wreck that can be made of human souls once they have assented to the first evil step. There is in this play no whisper of redemptive grace or of the possibility of repentance and a new start. It is all dark—nothing but deliberately planned sin bringing more sin, till the full cycle is achieved and the terrible avenging fury, herself damned, leaves the ruined lives and the wasted hopes to rot.

In *The Physicists,* which shows three world famous scientists who choose to be incarcerated in a mental hospital rather than to allow their scientific discoveries to destroy the world, Durrenmatt indicates that knowledge irresponsibly pursued as an end in itself, or as a tool to establish dominance over others, brings destruction. Human wisdom used solely as a means to wealth reduces man to a stinking, cowering wretch, subhuman, and in the end powerless to help himself. If we will this use of knowledge, we will also this terrible accomplishment of our aims, and we shall achieve our own destruction.

What are our deepest aims? This is, of course, a crucial question —a question fit to be asked at the foot of the Cross.

We know what our Lord's aim was—"To do the will of him who sent me"—to unself himself, so that God might be all. We know this as a verbal statement. How long have we ever spent in pondering what, *really,* it might mean if we came anywhere near understanding it—even for ourselves, even in the circumstances of our daily lives? What was recorded in that last mighty cry of our Lord was not that he had won any kind of tangible success; from whom, since he is God, should he have won it? No, success is not a condition for resurrection. But to the very end Christ went the way a man must walk "before you call him a man"—through the hard work of the successful ministry, through the incomprehension of his friends, right into the physical agony, and beyond into the void of the absence of God. And now he was past even that; the pain was almost over; only the perfected offering was there. His aim had been true. He had not missed the mark. He had shown that nothing, not height nor depth, not physical agony, not mental nor spiritual darkness, nor any other creature, can ever separate us from the love of God. Openness to the loving will of God, which brings with it the willingness to take whatever is coming to us out of the surrounding darkness, even if it seems that we must die with an unanswered question on our lips—that openness to the future is indeed a condition for resurrection.

Let us pray.

Lord, we are so often in a muddle.

We so often give up halfway because we have not spared time to examine in your presence what we are trying to do, and to ask you whether it is in accordance with your will for us. Help us to persevere in the undertakings which are worthwhile, and to relinquish without distress those which prove to have been mistaken, and let us always know that you blessed equally the activity of Martha and the stillness of Mary. And let us always give thanks to you for the achievements of great minds in your service.

Prevent us, O Lord, in all our doings with thy most gracious favor and further us with thy continual help; that in all our works, begun, continued, and ended in thee, we may glorify thy holy name, and finally by thy mercy obtain everlasting life; through Jesus Christ our Lord.

Let us keep silence.

VII

He had accomplished his mission. And if this had been a story of a hero-God—one of the Greek or Norse gods—what loud acclamation, what sunlit gatherings on Olympus, what feasting in Valhalla, what trumpets, what eagles, what fluttering gonfalons would have celebrated such a victory!

This departure is different.

> And now, beloved Lord, Thy soul resigning
> Into Thy Father's arms with conscious will,
> Calmly, with reverend grace, Thy head inclining,
> The throbbing brow and laboring breast grow still.

One has seen it happen at a death. The moment of total quiet before the heart stops beating, a sense of deep concentration of the almost extinct powers before what J. B. S. Haldane has called "the whirling darkness of anoxia" claims the dying body.

Here on Calvary there is still one thing left for the Lord to do. His human will is still under his own control. His spirit is still on active service. He has one last deed to perform before the ultimate end. He gives back to God with whom he was from the beginning the spirit which has been, as it were, on a proving trial —not proving, of course, to God, but proving to man what a man can be—and it has been proved flawless, without stain or inadequacy anywhere. With hardly a sigh our Lord resigns life here into the hands of that God who is blessed Trinity, Lord of all being. The journey has been made by our Master. When our time comes, we know we need not make it alone. He is ready and he accompanies us. In Campion's words:

Never weather-beaten sail more willing bent to shore,
Never tired Pilgrim's limbs affected slumber more,
Than my wearied sprite now longs to fly out of my troubled
    breast.
O come quickly, sweetest Lord, and take my soul to rest.

Christ, if we could but follow!

The unbelievable truth is that we can follow, but it takes a lifetime. And, quite honestly, most of us don't much care to make the effort as life gets past its peak. We prefer to settle for easy ways, familiar ways. And we tend to forget that if we really want to live and die with Christ—and we can't have the one without the other—we have to study living and dying all the way. Leonardo da Vinci said on his deathbed, "I thought I had been learning how to live but all the while I have been learning how to die." W. B. Yeats wrote:

An aged man is but a paltry thing,
A tattered coat upon a stick, unless
Soul clap its hands and sing, and louder sing
For every tatter in its mortal dress.

It is easy to say that no one really cares about the old nowadays; it is indeed a disgrace to us all that too many old people are too lonely. And one can get little direct guidance from the New Testament about how to grow old; it's all a record of youth. After all, Jesus' earthly life stopped at thirty-three years of age. Yet the aging and the old could do more themselves, perhaps, than they do, and we can be grateful to the young dramatist John Arden for his satirical comedy called *The Happy Haven* in its harsh, unsentimental presentation of the plight of old people. Arden shows us both the shockingly impersonal treatment of the old people in his play, which is set in a home for the aged, and also the real selfishness of old age. Who, in the later years of life, can avoid several uneasy pricks of conscience while listening to Arden's old Mrs. Phineus making her simple statement of wants?

> I'm an old old lady
> And I don't have long to live.
> I am only strong enough to take
> Not to give. No time left to give.
> I want to drink, I want to eat,
> I want my shoes taken off my feet. . . .
> I want to sleep but not to dream
> I want to play and win every game
> To live with love but not to love
> The world to move but me not to move
> I want I want for ever and ever
> The world to work, the world to
>   be clever.
> Leave me be, but don't leave me
>   alone.
> That's what I want. I'm a big
>   round stone
> Sitting in the middle of a thunder-
>   storm
> There you are: that's true.
> That's me. Now: you.

It isn't as beautiful a picture of old age as Campion's lovely poem, but it is painfully salutary! In normal circumstances it is rare, for most of us, that the last years or months of life provide much in the way of preparation for death. It is partly because such opportunity is rare that we value the account of the last days and hours of the modern martyrs whose letters from prison form the book called *Dying We Live.* Their courage is incredible, of course, but even more incredible is the way assurance grows as death approaches. Contemporary dramatists may well have felt unwilling to *invent* death scenes of this kind in an age where so many men and women have actually endured such deaths, so let us consider one passage from the real life drama of a teacher, executed in 1943 by the Gestapo in Plotzensee. His last letter contains these words:

A deep, liberating peace encircles me. An astounding emotion wells up in me and fills me wholly. The essential element in life and in man is not affected by death. My last plea is: Do not close yourself to the beauty of this world. Through your being, your art, your voice, create joy, happiness, kindness, peace.

> O strangely luminous life, so close to death,
> The great sleep hovers very near
> With its dark pinion overshadowing
> The blinding fires of wishes and of fears.

Over and over again in these letters from prison, the testimony is repeated—They *know* death is not the end.

Yet the approaches to death are often hard, and we are sometimes tempted to falsify the truth in our desire not to know how hard it is to reach death, how hard to bear with dignity and fortitude the humiliating failure of our powers, mental and physical. We do each other no service if, when the moment of death is near, we pretend it is still far off. What John Betjeman has called "the chintzy cheeriness" of the casual visitor to the sick person at home or in hospital can be a cruel addition to the sufferings of the mortally ill.

Shakespeare expresses this attitude with his usual profound understanding when he makes Mistress Quickly tell us of Falstaff's last moments. He presents the situation half-jocularly, but the deep compassion shows through as he intended it should. Mistress Quickly says in her account of how Falstaff died: "So a' cried out 'God, God, God!' three or four times. Now I, to comfort him, bid him a' should not think of God; I hoped there was no need to trouble himself with any such thoughts yet." Poor, lonely, sinful old man, always timid and now comfortless, alone with his sins. At least Mistress Quickly was there; he was not, as too many are, left without human hand at the last. But in the shallowness of her understanding of death she trivializes it, tries to bring the great mystery of the dark wings down to the level of a tiresome visitor. This kind of behavior brings no help to the dying. Perhaps it is to the group of disciples at the foot of the Cross that we must turn to know what is required of us.

Anyone who has ever been dangerously ill knows the relief brought by the friend who is willing to admit that the valley of the shadow, whichever turning we are to take, is real, is the place where we are. And it is often not so much a question of finding the right thing to say as of being willing to sit quietly, perhaps to listen, perhaps simply to "be there," knowing that one day we shall indeed "be there" ourselves. One need never be afraid of speaking too simply to the very ill. We are all grateful for being assured that beneath us are the everlasting arms and that our friends care what happens; but silent presence can be enough.

Perhaps this is the moment on Good Friday when we may most fitly remember the dead whom we have loved. Those who have lived their full tale of years, who have lived and died believing. Those who have died young, suddenly, violently, or from disease. Those who have died faithless. Those for whom life has seemed too hard, too cruel, too hopeless, and who have taken their own lives. Those whom we feel to be near us still and those who, however dearly we loved them, seem to have vanished utterly.

Before the unfathomable mystery of death let us commit our spirits and theirs into the hands of the God whose nature and whose name we know: "His nature and his name is Love."

To live—to practice living—in the realization of the *mystery* of life and death, the nearness of one to the other, the reality and yet the thinness of the veil that separates one from the other, and so to recognize the great cloud of witnesses in whose company we are—this surely is part of the way Christ went, part of our preparation for resurrection. And in practicing this realization age or youth are irrelevant.

Let us pray.

O God, giver of life, give us the courage to rejoice always in thy gift. Let us live fully, giving or receiving, till seeing thee as the pure flame of joy, we are called back to thee, and yield ourselves joyfully to thee, flame to flame.

Let us remember before God all who are near to death and all who care for the dying.

A prayer of the Abbé Fénelon

O my God, I leave myself in thy divine hands. Turn about this clay, turn it this way or that, according to thy pleasure. Give it a form, then if thou pleasest, break it in pieces. It is thine, it has nothing to say, it is enough that it answers thy purposes, and that nothing in it resists thy good pleasure for which it was created.

Let us keep silence.

CONCLUSION

He bowed his head and gave up his spirit.

And then, you remember, the centurion came and found Jesus
was already dead, and so contented himself with piercing the side
with a spear and did not break the legs. And then the brave
Joseph of Arimathea and the timid, apprehensive Nicodemus
came and took down the body and wrapped it and laid it in
Joseph's own new, rock-hewn tomb, and rolled a great stone in
front of it and went away. And that was that.

The crowds had dispersed. One Gospel says they went home
beating their breasts. Tradition reports curious events in the city
that evening: the dead rising from their sepulchers and walking
the streets, the elements, thunder and lightning, disturbed. Michel
de Ghelderode, in *The Women at the Tomb,* has made a powerful, though hideous, play out of the stories, showing us the utter
dismay and confusion and the bitter disillusionment of the disciples. Something, certainly, had happened, more than people had
bargained for when they set out that morning. The cosmic battle
between good and evil had been shown them in a way they had
not expected, and they thought it had all ended in darkness and
despair.

We are part of that crowd. Among us are writers, artists,
preachers, and teachers. Much prayer is needed for all who wrestle
intellectually with the ultimate problems of good and evil,
whether they be Christians or not. They are all, at varying levels,
forced to struggle with the deep realities of life, and it is probably
true to say that some of them lack joy as they wage their battles.
And we? We, the small minority group who profess Christianity?

Is this where we can help them, at this point of their joylessness?

We recollect that Good Friday observances have no meaning unless they brace us for the stern demands of a resurrection faith. And God the Holy Spirit may show us on this day something of what that faith demands of us.

By relating the Words from the Cross to the themes of today's drama it is possible to see that Christian and non-Christian are alike grappling with the central problems of the meaning and the demands of life. The commitment to follow the road Christ walked down means, at the very least, these things: The practice of forgiveness; the refusal to act or think thievishly in any way; the determination to care, far beyond the limits of the blood tie; the duty to satisfy the hunger and thirst, physical and spiritual, of others, and the duty to recognize our own thirst for God; the willingness to accept ignorance, darkness, and desolation; the necessity to examine our aims; the resolution to live so that death, however solemn, is never terrifying to us or our friends, and so that we remain ever open to the loving will of God; last of all, to follow Christ's demand of us—that we rejoice.

For we—it is the supreme privilege of the Christian faith— we wait now for Easter in the sure hope of Christ's triumph over sin. Is it possible that through the Christian hope, as it shines out of our own very ordinary lives, our world may take note that we have been with Jesus and that the resurrection life is a reality?

In the beginning was the Word; and in the end the Word abides—our Way, our Truth, our Life.

Amen. Even so, Lord Jesus, come.